Understanding
Islam™

Muslims Around the World Today

Philip Wolny

ROSEN
PUBLISHING®

New York

For Dévina Fitriyanti Azis and Lina Nadar

Published in 2009 by The Rosen Publishing Group, Inc.
29 East 21st Street, New York, NY 10010

Library of Congress Cataloging-in-Publication Data

Wolny, Philip.
Muslims around the world today / Philip Wolny.—1st ed.
    p. cm.—(Understanding Islam)
Includes bibliographical references and index.
ISBN-13: 978-1-4358-5067-5 (library binding)
ISBN-13: 978-1-4358-5385-0 (pbk)
ISBN-13: 978-1-4358-5389-8 (6 pack)
1. Islam—21st century. 2. Muslims—Europe. 3. Muslims—North America. 4. Islam and state—Islamic countries. 5. Ummah (Islam) I. Title.
BP161.3.W65 2008
297.09'0511—dc22
                                                      2008014188

Manufactured in the United States of America

On the cover: (*Top left*) Muslim teenager Sarah Ismail attends an electronic music class at Sharon High School, in Sharon, Massachusetts. (*Bottom right*) Indonesian Muslims join in prayer at the start of Eid al-Adha celebrations at the Istiqlal Mosque in Jakarta, Indonesia.

Contents

Introduction

Islam is one of the world's fastest-growing religions. Many non-Muslims, however, may know little about it. It is the world's second-largest faith after Christianity, and Muslims have made invaluable contributions to the sciences, art, culture, and politics in the course of world history.

Muslims around the world—from countries like Indonesia, Iran, and Algeria, to American cities like New York City; Dearborn, Michigan; and Toledo, Ohio—are an amazingly diverse group. Like the many different faith groups within Christianity and Judaism, Muslims worship in many ways. Aside from the two main branches of Islam, Sunni and Shia, there are also many smaller groups, or sects. While there are some Muslims who are very devout (those who take their religion very seriously and strictly), there are also Muslims who are loosely religious—that is, the religion itself is not a central part of their lives. Not all

Muslims today, such as this woman on a mobile phone outside the Mosque of Sultan Ahmet I in Istanbul, Turkey, live in a world where modernity and deep religious tradition exist side by side.

Muslims pray five times a day or fast during the holy month of Ramadan, but they still consider themselves Muslim.

Muslims live in states such as Saudi Arabia and Iran where religious authorities actively shape the policies of the government, as well as in countries like Turkey where the government is secular and resists the presence of religious viewpoints in politics. In most Muslim-majority countries, secular governments tend to be highly authoritarian, inspiring popular support for opposition political parties that promise to introduce Islamic values of justice, democracy, and equality into government. Others live in the West: North America, Europe, and Australia, for example. There, Muslims are a minority but generally enjoy religious freedom and participation in culture and politics.

Unfortunately, Muslims face challenges wherever they live. Some Muslims live in states that are undemocratic, while those in the West often encounter fear and discrimination because of stereotypes and because of unfamiliar dress or customs. The September 11, 2001, terrorist attacks, as well as other attacks by Islamist extremists in Madrid, London, Bali, and other parts of Indonesia have inspired fear and hatred of Muslims, making some consider all adherents of the faith to be extremists or religious fanatics.

But learning about how Muslims live their lives is the best way to change fear of Islam into understanding and appreciation. In this book, you will meet members of a worldwide Islamic community and learn how they manage to fit in with their non-Muslim neighbors. You will also learn how they view such issues as fundamentalism, moderation, and secular life.

Indonesia: A Nation of Contrasts

I magine you are walking down a street in Jakarta, Indonesia's capital. You encounter two women passing by. One wears a skirt, sandals, and a T-shirt, the other a traditional head scarf and robe. Which one do you think is a practicing Muslim? With approximately 85 percent of Indonesia's 225 million people identified as Muslims, it's likely that both are.

Most Indonesians are Sunni Muslims, though many forms of Islam peacefully coexist in Indonesia. It has a reputation as a moderate Islamic democracy. As with any religion, there are a wide range of Muslims. On one end of the spectrum, there are those who are strict and very conservative. On the other end of the spectrum are the extremely liberal, non-practicing Muslims who consider Islam as simply part of their cultural identity. Mainstream Muslims, typically holding moderate religious, social, and political views, span the broad middle. As elsewhere throughout the world, there is no one way to be Muslim in

Indonesia. Rather, there are almost an infinite number of ways to mingle religion, culture, and society.

Asia Pacific: A Unique Tapestry of Islamic Faith

Though the largest Islamic nation, Indonesia is one of several countries in the Asia Pacific region with Muslim populations. There are Muslim minorities in the Philippines, Thailand, and Australia. Malaysia, Indonesia's neighbor, is a constitutional monarchy with Islam as the official state religion. Malaysia, like Indonesia, recognizes freedom of religion, making these two nations different from a country like Saudi Arabia, where people of non-Muslim faiths can find it difficult to worship.

In addition, thousands of islands in this region of the world have developed their own unique mixtures of religions and peoples. One of Indonesia's most popular destinations, Bali, is mainly Hindu. On other islands, Muslims and Christians live together peacefully. In some places, there may be conflict, however. In Indonesia, a growing minority of conservative Muslims is pushing for stricter rules in several regions. Some groups, often characterized as Islamists because they want to implement strict Islamic religious law, called Sharia, have become more prominent in recent years.

The Push for Sharia Law

Some of Indonesia's many regions are becoming more conservative than in the past, passing legislation based on certain interpretations of Islamic laws and regulations. Take, for example, the small village of Bulukumba, located

A veiled *algojo*, an official that enforces Sharia law in certain parts of Indonesia, administers a public caning to thirty-year-old Nasrul Mubin as punishment for a gambling offense.

on the eastern Indonesian island of Sulawesi. According to a February 2007 report by *Time* magazine, Bulukumba passed rules influenced by Sharia law. Alcohol is now illegal; modest clothes are required; alms, or charitable contributions, are mandatory; and students and people who want to marry must show ability to read the Qur'an in Arabic.

Village chief Andi Rukman Abdul Jabbar also declared that gambling, drinking, and adultery should be punished by caning. Three citizens have been caned, while another has been banished from the village. Females must wear head scarves when entering Jabbar's office. Jabbar says these laws are helping his citizens. "In 2005, we used to have an incidence of theft almost every day, but not anymore," he told *Time*.

Other Indonesians oppose the push for Sharia-based rules, seeing it as evidence of negative, foreign influence. Much of the conservative movement is based on stricter forms of Islam, like Wahhabism and Salafism, which are more prevalent in the Middle East and nations like Pakistan and Afghanistan.

These rules have caused problems and confusion in some areas. In February 2006, Lilies Landawati, a thirty-five-year-old mother of two, was walking home from work after dark in Tanggerrang, a city near Jakarta. "I was grabbed by five people as I was standing on the side of the street," she told Bloomberg News. "I thought I was being abducted." It turned out that Landawati had run afoul of a recent local law that said women out alone at night had to prove that they were not prostitutes. Held overnight, she was fined thirty-four dollars, which she would be required to pay to avoid serving a three-day jail sentence. Unable to pay the fine for financial as well as more reasons, she told Bloomberg that if she did pay the fine, it would be "the same thing as admitting I'm a prostitute."

Two of a Kind

Not too far away, but perhaps worlds apart, there is the multiethnic and multireligious stew of Jakarta. For resident Julia Suryakusuma, an Indonesian journalist, religion is a question of personal choice. In a speech given at the University of Melbourne Law School in Melbourne, Australia, and reprinted on Australiansall.com, she described how her friendship with a more traditional Muslim woman sometimes surprised others. For Suryakusuma, "Being a Muslim in Indonesia, you don't have to look a certain way. There's no rule, nothing in the Koran, that says you have to wear a particular outfit or hat to win God's approval."

Suryakusuma comes from a liberal upbringing. She has long hair and often wears jewelry, makeup, and fashionable, tighter-fitting clothing. Her friend Neng, on the other hand, comes from a more Islam-centered background and dresses

A few days before the *Eid ul-Fitr* festival that marks the end of Ramadan, a market vendor in Jakarta, Indonesia, prepares the beef that customers will consume to celebrate the end of their month of daily fasting.

in loose clothing and wears a hijab, or head scarf. However, "It's not culture and ethnicity that makes us close, but intellectual and spiritual connections [as well as] an appetite for knowledge and a belief in democracy," Suryakusuma said.

Faith or Exclusion?

The growing conservative Islamic movement in Indonesia has even come up in Suryakusuma's family life. Once, her husband brought her mother some chicken from Australia. She was surprised days later that her mother had not touched it because Suryakusuma's brother, who had become more religiously conservative in recent years, had doubted that the chicken was halal. Halal refers to specific ways of killing and preparing certain animals according to established rules that many Muslims adhere to. Halal is very similar to the kosher rules that govern observant Jews' food preparation and consumption.

For Suryakusuma's mother, who is not conservative herself, her son's opinion seemed to win out in the end because he seemed more devout. But in light of his views on a variety of issues, Suryakusuma believes that her brother's path is "one of exclusion." She looks to her friend Neng for inspiration because of her ability to juggle traditional values with the challenges of living in the fast-paced and often materialistic modern world, using spirituality as her guide.

Deep Roots

It is especially in out-of-the-way places in Indonesia that Islam has adapted locally in unique ways. In remote areas, ancient traditions of belief in animal spirits (animism),

Priests at a temple in Besakih, Bali, bless the food of pilgrims. While Bali is primarily Hindu, Indonesia has many religious minorities and many ways of approaching Islam, including using elements of pre-Islamic faiths in their worship.

along with aspects of Buddhism, Hinduism, and even Christianity, blend with Islam.

Take the island of Lombok, inhabited by the Sasak ethnic group, for example. Though Muslims, they also have a caste system, much like Hindus, where Sasak children are born into one of four castes, or groups. They live comfortably with the centuries old Buddhist minority on the island and are known for being quite tolerant of other groups.

Then there's the village of Tenggulun on the island of Java. The village chief, Maksun, a Muslim, is also a traditional faith healer. "I am a good Muslim, but I am also a paranormal," he told *Time* magazine in September 2004. Such traditions exist throughout Indonesia. Muslim leaders in the city of Solo, for example, oversee an annual pageant of sacred objects, with albino water buffalos (considered supernatural animals) leading the way.

Maksun's village, Tenggulun, is also known as a center for activism and militancy. Some Muslims consider his mix of Islam and traditional ways an insult. A local Muslim named Mohammad Zakaria leads a local boarding school, or pesantren, and is far stricter in his beliefs. For example, Maksun may visit a tomb of a famous scholar to receive answers to prayers, which Zakaria's students would consider blasphemous. Mostly, the traditional Indonesians live and let live with the Muslims who have adopted stricter inter- pretations of their faith. Yet, some traditional Indonesians are troubled by such changes in the region. Maksun says of the more conservative Muslims, "Their ideology is not suitable to local people . . . They don't agree with many of our traditions that we have practiced for hundreds of years."

Terror in Indonesia

There is a small minority of Muslims, however, that seeks to push the entire country toward its extreme interpretations of Islam and militant worldview and feels justified in using violent means to do so. Some are rumored to have ties to Al Qaeda, a militant group that has claimed responsibility for the 9/11 attacks. In 2002, the Indonesian militant group Jemaah Islamiyah killed 202 people in nightclub bombings in Bali. That, and later bombings in 2005, have inspired heated debate. The *Economist* wrote in January 2008 that

A Muslim woman waves the Indonesian flag in 2003 during celebrations of the fifty-eighth anniversary of Indonesia's gaining independence from Dutch colonial rule. Though Islam is not the state religion, an estimated 85 percent of Indonesians are observant Muslims.

about 10 percent of Indonesians thought that terrorism was permissible if done "to protect the faith." The vast majority of Indonesians, however, condemn such actions.

Moderation and Modernity

Dévina Fitriyanti Azis, a student of Indonesian Muslim descent studying in Brussels, Belgium, has spent time in Indonesia, where her family comes from, and France, where she was brought up. While Islam is very important to them, she says that Indonesians value their national identity and shared beliefs just as much as their religious identity.

Azis also agrees that moderation wins out in Indonesia, despite all the news about the rise of conservative Islam there. "The Muslims in Indonesia are moderate," she asserted in an interview with the author, "though the media only talk about the fundamentalist ones. Women have an important role to play in the society. While having a female head of state is still a taboo in some Western countries, Indonesia had its first female president in 2001."

The question of traditional clothing is an important matter for Indonesians, but Azis says there is more to this issue than meets the eye: "A lot of women are indeed wearing the veil, but it does not necessarily represent their total devotion to God, especially when [they're] wearing tight clothes. The veil is also a fashion accessory, as well as a hat." Furthermore, many Muslim women do not see the veil as a symbol of tradition but as an active part of their Muslim identity in the modern world.

Iran: The Islamic Republic

When people think about Islam, they often think of the Middle East. When Islam began to spread from the seventh century onward, it was the peoples of this area of the world that became the first Muslims. In the modern era, the Middle East is home to long-standing traditional forms of Islam. Due to the social structures and political history of the region in the post-colonial era, Muslim societies in this region often exhibit relatively conservative attitudes.

Islam's Heartland

The most sacred sites of the Muslim faith are found in the Middle East. For example, Muslims face Mecca in Saudi Arabia when they pray. Millions of the faithful make at least one pilgrimage to the holy city of Mecca (where the prophet Muhammad was born, lived much of his early life, and began to share the teachings of what would become the Islamic faith). This pilgrimage is called the hajj.

Much of the Middle East is Sunni. There are Shia as well, especially in Iran, where they make

The courtyard outside the Grand Mosque in Mecca, Saudi Arabia, Islam's holiest center and destination, serves as a gathering place for huge crowds just before the annual hajj, or pilgrimage.

up 90 percent of the people, and Iraq, where they may make up as much as 60 percent. In each nation and region, Muslims exhibit differing tribal and family structures, languages, dialects, and lifestyles. Muslims have vibrant, highly individual cultures in the tiny, oil-rich nation of Oman with its gleaming skyscrapers; the poorer neighborhoods of Cairo, Egypt; and the small villages of the Arabian Peninsula. Just as any other place in the world, the inhabitants of this region are balancing the characteristics and needs of modern life with the wisdom of a culture that is many centuries old.

The Islamic Republic of Iran

Even though the majority of Muslims in the Middle East are Sunni, Iran's population is 90 percent Shia. Iran is a complex nation, often in the news because of its differences with the West and its strained relationship with the United States. In fact, it is a place where the Islamic faith and the rich cultural traditions of Persia have combined in a unique fashion. In recent years, Iranians, like others around the world, have also absorbed influences from Western culture.

Iran is a unique modern "religious state," where religious authorities play a powerful role in the government's leadership and decisions. Religious elders called mullahs (the name for Muslim clerics or mosque leaders in Iran, Turkey, and parts of Asia), who in the past tended to distance themselves from politics, have exercised a great deal of power in the decades following the Iranian Revolution in 1979. Young Iranians, many of whom do not share the prior generation's views on government, seek to change and redefine what the

Iran's Sunnis

While Iran is the largest majority-Shia nation, there are millions of Iranians who are not Shia. The Sunni minority, many of whom live near Iran's border with Iraq, is one of those groups. Approximately 9 or 10 percent of Iranians are Sunni, including most Kurds, Baluchis, and Turkmen. Tensions exist among some Shia and Sunni groups in Iran. Generally speaking, however, there is little conflict between the two sects because any conflict that occurs is usually a result of economic, tribal, or ethnic competition rather than religious difference. Although Iran's constitution recognizes the rights of Sunnis, it still prevents them from becoming the supreme leader or president.

In Iran's southeastern Sistan-Baluchistan province, a group called Jundullah has carried out terrorist attacks against Shi'as and has taken hostages. Jundullah claims it fights for the rights of Sunnis and Baluchis who feel that they are discriminated against both for their religion and ethnicity. Because of its Sunni roots, Jundullah has been accused by the Iranian government of being closely linked with Al Qaeda, also a Sunni-based movement.

notion of an "Islamic republic" means. Like Indonesia and Turkey, Iran has democratic elections and institutions, yet religious authorities have the final say on matters of policy. Those who are pushing for change face many challenges in shifting the nature of Iranian politics, but they are hopeful that they will eventually prevail.

Islamic Revolution

After many decades, the ruthless and dictatorial shah of Iran, Mohammad Reza Pahlavi, was removed from power during the Iranian Revolution of 1979. This hugely popular movement, which included leading intellectuals, many university students, and middle-class merchants, replaced the shah's secular dictatorship with a government that adhered to Islamic law.

Ayatollah Ruhollah Khomeini, leader of the Iranian Islamic revolution, is pictured here thronged by admiring supporters on February 2, 1979, after returning to Iran from a fifteen-year exile.

The new rulers were also very much against Western influences, especially the United States, which had supported the shah. They tried to eliminate provocative clothing, Hollywood films, and other things considered un-Islamic and corrupting. Religious leaders gained influence over government policies and eliminated the secular participants in the revolution. Ruhollah Khomeini, a member of the highest-ranking group of Shia religious scholars known as ayatollahs, was recognized as the supreme leader of Iran following the ouster of the shah.

The Iranian Revolution was also important around the world. Many activists advocated the revolutionary and sometimes violent overthrow of dictatorships throughout the Muslim world. They sought to replace them with Islamic-styled governments that they believed would restore Muslim sovereignty and dignity, reduce Western cultural influences, and introduce justice and other Islamic values in governance.

A Silent Revolution

Nearly as important to Iranians as being Muslim is their Persian heritage. Iran and its surrounding areas were once part of the mighty, pre-Islamic Persian Empire. Iranian Shiites are greatly influenced by Persian traditions, some of which go back 2,500 years. Though Iran's religious rulers tried for years to ban or limit traditional Persian practices they considered un-Islamic, they have had to come to terms with Iranians' cultural pride and the continuity of these practices.

Happy New Year, Iranian Style

In March 2006, the *New York Times* reported on the Iranian New Year celebrations, *Nowruz*, in the city of Isfahan. *Chahar Shanbeh Suri*, celebrated just before *Nowruz*, is a holiday with roots in pre-Islamic Persian history that is marked by fireworks and jumping over small fires to promote good health in the coming year. Despite years of resistance, the government recently reserved special parks where Iranians could celebrate. A local tailor, identified only as Akbar to protect his identity, told the *Times*, "They really tried to take away *Nowruz* from people . . . People are turning away from religion altogether. They are not listening to what the government is saying."

While it seems highly unlikely that Iranians are turning away from religion, there does seem to be a trend away from the influence of religious authorities. Most Iranians believe that Islam and Iran's rich pre-Islamic traditions can coexist. Isfahan Baker Jaafar Hemmassian told the *Times*, "Iranians have both tradition and religion, and both get respected in return . . . All of the traditions of *Nowruz* are accepted by Islam."

Saxophonist Masoud Ahmadzadeh plays a tune for the patrons of a Tehran cafe, an activity most likely frowned upon by some strict mullahs.

Looking Westward

Unlike during the charged atmosphere of the decade following the Iranian Revolution, during which the Iran-Iraq War took place, Iranian youth today seem to be living their lives more freely, in increasing defiance of official rules and restrictions. PBS's *Frontline* reported in 2006 that Valentine's Day, officially banned by the government, had become popular among young people. In fact, it has become a huge event, second only to *Nowruz* in how much business it generates.

Unlike the stricter, older ayatollahs, young people's attitudes toward change are very open. While unheard of years ago, unmarried men and women now socialize together in coffee shops or share a meal for Valentine's Day. Shifting norms due to Western influence and globalization are evident in Iran as elsewhere. These are viewed favorably by some and unfavorably by others. At a cocktail party in Tehran, Iran's capital city, in July 2007, a reporter from the *Economist* met women in revealing dresses and men in Western designer styles, all drinking alcohol. One young woman asked, "Why can't people in the West see what Iran is really like? We're the future." Of course, there are other Iranians who do not approve of such a "Westernized" lifestyle being adopted—especially those aspects that violate religious teachings—but who are open-minded and welcome better relations with the West based on an attitude of mutual respect.

Muslims in Western Europe

If you stroll through the neighborhoods of many European cities, you encounter sights, sounds, and scents unimaginable there decades ago. Women in colorful head scarves, the distinct rhythms of North African music, and the unique aromas of sizzling halal meat greet you. Enter some areas of Berlin, London, or Paris, and it feels like you've entered another world, where you are just as likely to hear Arabic, Turkish, and many other languages alongside German, English, and French.

The U.S. State Department estimates that thirteen million Muslims live in western Europe, most of them in the countries making up the European Union (EU). Most arrived in the second half of the twentieth century as immigrants, largely from lands that were formerly European colonies: Indonesia, India, Pakistan, North Africa, and the Middle East. A great many were guest workers who relocated to Europe. It was expected by many of the "host" countries

British policemen guard a street closed off to accommodate a group of Muslims praying.

that they would eventually return to where they came from. But it did not quite turn out that way.

Muslims throughout Europe in the twentieth and twenty-first centuries have faced challenges unlike those in majority-Muslim nations like Iran and Indonesia. They, like other immigrants from Asia, Africa, and elsewhere, were strangers in a strange land, seemingly quite different from native Europeans. Many faced discrimination, even violence. Some found the increasingly secular cultures of their new countries quite alien and had to get used to a new way of life.

Still, the story of Islam in Europe spans centuries. We will now examine the Muslim immigrant experience in England, Germany, and France. The rich contributions of North African Moors to Spanish culture and the influence of the Ottoman Turks to eastern European cultures are still visible today. While much of the news about European Muslims centers on western Europe, eastern Europe has had Muslim populations for centuries. From art and architecture, to music and cuisine, it is difficult to say that Islam is "foreign" to Europe.

Terror on European Soil

After 9/11, Europe has had its own terrorist tragedies, making many Europeans fear the "foreigners" among them. Muslim militants killed 191 people in train bombings in Madrid, Spain, on March 11, 2004. Suicide bombers killed at least fifty-five people in a series of coordinated attacks centering on London's King's Cross station on July 7, 2005, the first suicide bombing ever to occur in England.

Terrorism is nothing new in Europe. In Spain, separatists of the Basque region have waged deadly terrorist attacks for years. Great Britain experienced extreme violence and bloodshed during the decades-long "Troubles" between Catholic and Protestant populations in Northern Ireland and the British army stationed there (theoretically to keep the peace, though its forces really supported the Protestant establishment).

What made the 2005 London bombings even more frightening was that the bombers seemed like normal young Britons, not extremists. They were of Pakistani descent, born and bred in the city of Leeds, England. One had dressed in flashy, youthful clothing. Another passed up an arranged marriage by his family to instead date a non-Muslim woman at his university. It seemed that all of the men had been attracted to extremism for different reasons and had shocked their parents and everyone else by their actions.

England

After World War II, large groups of people from India and the newly formed nation of Pakistan moved to England to work (both India and Pakistan were former colonies of Great Britain). Of these, almost all of the Pakistanis were Muslim, while a majority of the Indians were Hindu. Many of them and their descendants consider themselves to be British first and foremost. Yet, cultural and religious differences, prejudices exhibited by Britons toward immigrants, and Muslim sympathy for the plight of their co-religionists caught up in global political struggles have caused some Muslims to feel marginalized and angry toward Western powers.

The Backlash Against Muslims

Much like the climate of fear in the United States after 9/11, the suspicion and fear held by the non-Muslim majority were a challenge for Muslims everywhere in Europe. But a poll published around the time of the London bombings showed that as little as 4 percent of British Muslims felt it was "acceptable for religious or political groups to use violence for political ends." The London bombing incident was a reminder to the British Muslim community that it, too, needed to keep an eye out for extremism in its ranks.

Integration and Tradition

A Muslim teenager in London is just as likely to have a strong regional English accent as he is to pray five times daily. He may attend a British school and have the same hobbies and problems as other British teens. Muslims of all ages and backgrounds have approached integration into British society in different ways. Some become less devout, intermarry, and adopt a more "mainstream" Western lifestyle. Many have also rediscovered their religion and cultural heritage.

Take Shaista Aziz, an educated London woman who wrote for BBC News about her choice to wear the hijab (head scarf). She decided to wear the scarf as a statement of identity, following a personal quest to educate herself about Islam. After September 11, 2001, she considered it important to show her Muslim identity. "I have found a great deal of strength wearing the hijab," she wrote. She also finds it to be a way to bond with her fellow female Muslims, whether on the streets of London or with Muslim women worldwide. "Within Islam, there is a wealth of diversity," she pointed out. "The way Muslim women dress differs from country to country, [and] the way a Muslim woman wears a hijab may also differ."

A Cultural Divide

However, not everyone is ready to accept Muslim attire in every case. Controversy erupted in England when one

"discrimination is a growth industry"
frances gibb

A billboard in Birmingham, England, confronts anti-Muslim fear and stereotypes in a neighborhood where antiterror raids resulted in the arrest of nine Muslim men accused of planning kidnappings.

teaching assistant in Yorkshire, England, refused to take off her niqab, a full-face veil exposing only the eyes. She made sure to wear it in front of all male teachers. Her non-Muslim coworkers felt that hiding her face in an educational environment was inappropriate.

Most Westerners are used to seeing someone's face, whether it be a teacher, a person serving coffee, or a civil servant at the employment office. Some even see the niqab as a garment that oppresses women by hiding their faces.

But supporters of the Yorkshire woman say that her firing was discriminatory. They argue that the niqab actually liberates women from the need to wear makeup or a certain wardrobe and from unwanted attention from men. Such cases raise important new questions about the competing rights and cultural norms in societies that profess to value pluralism and freedom.

France: Compromise and Conflict

Mouhad Bourouis, a thirty-three-year-old attorney and son of Algerian immigrants, once worked at a day camp for underprivileged children in southern France. There were eighty children, and twenty-eight were Muslim. Ham and other kinds of pork were part of the usual meals, which the Muslim kids could not eat due to halal dietary restrictions. Bourouis informed all the parents that he would make meals that all the children could eat. "If they [non-Muslim campers] really wanted to eat sausage, they could wait to be back at the family dinner table," he told *Newsweek* in December 2007. Bourouis viewed his solution as a straightforward, simple, and effective compromise. For many others, however, such "accomodations" are outside the norms of mainstream French society.

Religion and Identity

The Muslim population in France is the largest in Europe—about six million, by some accounts. Of this number, around seven hundred thousand are considered observant Muslims. French Muslims mainly have roots in North

African nations like Algeria, Tunisia, and Morocco (countries formerly colonized by France). A majority of them celebrate only major holidays and events, their Muslim identity really showing during weddings, funerals, and traditional festivals, much like nominal Christians today who step into a church only for weddings, baptisms, Christmas, and Easter.

French, but Not French

Years ago, it was more common for North Africans to be labeled "Arabs." Now, they are known more as Muslims and refer to themselves as such. Though some are middle or upper class, a great majority are poor and live in segregated housing projects (*banlieues*) that surround big cities like Paris. They are places of high crime and unemployment, and, for young men, police harassment is common. The death of two youths fleeing police in November 2005 sparked riots throughout France.

Escaping the *banlieues* is not so simple, either. French Muslim job seekers often complain of discrimination. It is a painful dilemma because most simply want to be part of mainstream French society, but they feel like strangers within their own country. Adbelwaheb Bakli, the president of Muslim Youth of France, told the BBC, "If on one hand, you tell people that they are French, but on the other hand treat them as outsiders, young men in search of an identity will feel lost . . . They are expected to get [university] degrees, but in the end they face a wall." Lack of employment and disdain of their religious identity by some French people are cited by Muslims as major reasons for disaffection and uncertainty regarding Muslim integration in French society.

The Head Scarf Affair

In 1989, the issue of wearing the hijab in French schools first arose when three girls were expelled for wearing it in Creil, north of Paris. Since then, schools and the French government have sent mixed signals as to what is and is not permissible. The French have very strict rules regarding their form of secularism (called *laïcité*). In March 2004, the French parliament banned visible religious symbols in schools, including Jewish yarmulkes or large Christian crosses. Many Muslims, however, saw the law as being directed at hijabs in particular and took it as evidence that France feared its Muslims citizens.

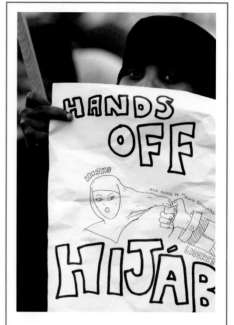

A Muslim woman at a January 17, 2003, protest outside the French Embassy in London holds up a sign that criticizes the French ban on religious symbols in schools, including the hijab.

French-Indonesian student Dévina Fitriyanti Azis, whom we met in chapter 1, agreed that the French reaction is a complicated one: "It is obvious that one should adapt a bit to the country and the culture one lives in, but on the other hand, the country should also attempt to rethink its society according to its inhabitants. If French people knew more about people's religions, they would not be afraid of them."

The Alevis

Sometimes, even something as seemingly innocent as a television program can upset people. An episode of the popular German show *Tatort* ("Crime Scene") caused protests when it dealt with sensitive issues in an Alevi Muslim family. Alevi Muslims are a mystical sect of Shia Muslims and a minority in Germany, making up about 10 percent of Germany's Muslim population. The majority of German Muslims are Sunni. On December 30, 2007, as many as twenty thousand Alevis protested in Cologne, Germany, against the show.

One protestor told Spiegel Online, "It's possible that Germans have no prejudice against us. But a film like this can aggravate tension in the Turkish community between Alevis and Sunnis." The Alevis have historically been more liberal than many Turkish Muslims—for example, men and women pray together. Old stereotypes from the days of the Ottoman Turks still exist, including an unfounded idea that Alevis tolerate incest. Alevis were hurt by their portrayal on the show and feared tensions would rise between them and other Turkish Muslims. One Alevi leader pointed out, "The Alevis respect freedom of press and freedom of opinion and are opposed to any ban on cultural expression. But these values must not be used to harm the dignity of a minority."

On June 16, 2007, a local right-wing group called Pro Cologne mobilized to oppose the building of a new, large mosque in Cologne, Germany.

Germany: The "Guest Workers" Who Stayed

Most of Germany's Muslims, estimated at anywhere between 3 and 3.5 million, are ethnic Turks. Many of their parents came years ago as guest workers (*gastarbeiter* in German) after World War II. For many years, there has been a push from these residents to gain full citizenship.

For decades, it was hard for anyone who didn't have German blood to become a full-fledged citizen. While this is changing, it is an emotional issue for German Muslims. One Muslim Turk, Yueksal Tuncay, told BBC News, "When I meet an official or a policeman, they see my black hair, and, to them, I am still a foreigner."

A German Mosque Sparks Controversy

Muslims in Cologne were excited when they heard about plans for a large mosque there. Diyant Isleri Turk-Islam Birligi (DITIB; in English, the Turkish Islamic Union for Religious Affairs), one of Germany's most important Muslim organizations, was behind the effort. In DITIB's current mosque, overcrowding is so great that worshippers often have to put prayer rugs in the parking lot and listen to services by loudspeaker.

Cologne is also one of Germany's most Roman Catholic cities. Tensions between ethnic Germans, especially Catholics, and the city's estimated Muslim population of 120,000 have risen since the mosque was announced. One DITIB worshipper, Mehmet Orman, told the Associated Press, "Of course, we need a big, representative mosque in this country."

But some groups are against the mosque or want it greatly reduced in size. They want to preserve Cologne's Catholic image and identity and fear Islamic fundamentalism. A right-wing group, Pro Cologne, has even collected eighteen thousand names in a petition against the mosque. Mehmet Yildirim, director of DITIB, called this reaction "racist and insulting," also telling the Associated Press, "We shouldn't have to justify ourselves that we need a house of prayer in Germany."

Turkey: Between East and West

On April 29, 2007, an estimated one million Turks marched in the streets of Istanbul, Turkey's capital. The protestors waved Turkish flags and carried portraits of Mustafa Kemal Ataturk, who founded the modern Turkish state in the 1920s. They were anxious about the possible election of Abdullah Gul to the presidency. Gul and the prime minister, Tayyip Erdogan, belong to the ruling Justice and Development Party (Adalet ve Kalkinma Partisi, or AKP). The protesters were worried that the party, which is popular among committed Turkish Muslims, would reverse the separation between religion and government that Ataturk instituted along European lines.

Turkey is a secular democracy, and about 98 percent of its seventy million citizens are Muslim. Since its founding after the fall of the Ottoman Empire following World War I, secular Turks have strongly resisted religious influence in Turkey's laws and government. Gul's wife regularly wore a hijab, and the protestors thought this was a symbol of what the AK party was truly loyal to: a push toward Islam-based governance. David Barchard, a veteran expert on Islam who lives in Ankara, Turkey, told Radio Free Europe that the protestors "don't want to live in a society like the Arab world . . . These people want Turkey to remain a secular society."

A Nation Seeking Balance

In Istanbul's Nisantasi district, with its fashionable cafes, expensive stores, and hip bars, the most Westernized Turks can be found at work and play. They think of their country as a modern state, a country that could be just as much a part of Europe as it is a part of Asia and the Muslim world.

As one woman told the BBC, "You can be a religious person, but you can also lead a very modern life." A recent BBC poll found that 91 percent of Turks say, "We are religious people." Still, more than half describe themselves as moderate. An overwhelming 85 percent also believe that someone who does not pray regularly can still be considered a Muslim. Turks, like most other Muslims, believe each person is individually accountable before God for fulfilling religious obligations, and the state should not become involved in personal spiritual matters.

Where Faith Runs Deep

In many parts of the countryside, however, and in many neighborhoods of Istanbul, Turks live in a more traditional and religious atmosphere distinct from Nisantasi's cosmopolitan. Near the important Fatih mosque, you are more likely to find women wearing head scarves and men with beards. While many very faithful Muslims are native to Istanbul, there have been many newcomers from the countryside in recent years. For them, the local mosque, daily prayers, and strict observance provide a sense of community in a strange, new place.

For all the fears of secularized Turks regarding the growing sense of Islamic identity expressed by other Turks, a general atmosphere of tolerance is evident in society. Some political parties wish to see more Islamic values balancing the extreme forms of secularism advocated by rival groups, but they do not advocate Sharia law itself as a basis for policy making. While the holy

On April 29, 2007, demonstrators in Istanbul protest the presidential candidacy of Abdullah Gul of the AK party, whom they believe will weaken secularism in Turkey.

month of Ramadan is an important time for the religiously observant, not all Turks fast from sunrise to sundown. There are also those who do not pray throughout the year, though they may observe Ramadan and other religious holidays. As in most societies, there is a wide spectrum of religiosity among the populace.

The Alevis: Turkey's Largest Minority

Whatever their degree of faith, Turkish Muslims are divided in other ways. You may encounter Turks who pray five

39

times daily, abstain from alcohol, and dress very modestly, as well as those who are more liberal in their dress and the practicing of their faith. Even among practicing Muslims, there can be great differences.

Alevi Muslims are a more liberal sect of Shia Muslims and Turkey's largest religious minority. They make up about 15 percent of the population. According to Izzetin Dogan, an Alevi spiritual leader who spoke with Network Europe News, the main principles of Alevis are rooted in a philosophy of loving God and one's fellow man, rather than being strict with rules. The Alevis have historically been more liberal than many Turkish Muslims—for example, men and women pray together.

Alevis do not observe Ramadan, and they are sometimes criticized for this. A child in school may be scolded by his teacher for not fasting. Some Alevis merely observe Ramadan so as not to cause trouble or generate intolerant attitudes in their neighbors or friends. One man at the Uskudar mosque told Network Europe News, "They don't fit in with us . . . they have funny ideas and are not real Muslims . . . Don't get me wrong, I am not prejudiced, some of my friends are Alevi, but I would never let my daughter marry one."

Turkey's Own Head Scarf Controversy

Though Turkey is a Muslim-majority nation, its laws separating religion and state are quite strong and absolute. Attempts to ban head scarves in schools, usually considered

Three women—two dressed in modest attire reflecting Islamic traditions, and one in more typically Western clothing—take a look at mobile phones in an Istanbul storefront display.

a western European phenomenon, first arose in Turkey. In 1987, secularists pressured the government's Higher Education Council to ban head coverings in universities. Protests by thousands of students and supporters followed. Eventually, many schools did not abide by the ban, but the issue has since continued to divide many Turks as a symbol of their views on the proper role of the state in protecting religious freedom versus sponsoring religion.

The flag of Turkey (*right*) flies alongside the flag of the European Union (EU) before an Istanbul mosque on October 4, 2005.

Turkey: A Member of the European Union?

Over the last few years, Turkey's government has been negotiating with the European Union (EU), seeking entry as a member state. Many Europeans believe that having Turkey join the union would be positive and that including a large Muslim democracy would do much to bring the West and the Islamic world together. Because of its unique history, religion, and culture, however, other Europeans think Turkey would not be a good fit with the EU.

Even Turks themselves are divided. In September 2007, the German Marshall Fund of the United States and an Italian foundation, Compagnia di San Paolo, released a poll showing that only 40 percent of Turks thought EU membership would be a good thing. In 2006, 54 percent of Turks had thought so, down from 73 percent in 2004. It remains uncertain how this unique Muslim nation will fit in with its western and eastern neighbors in the future and in which direction it will tend to drift.

The United States: Freedom and Fear

Not far from Detroit, the city of Dearborn, Michigan is, in many ways, like any American city. In some areas you will see churches, diners, and fast-food restaurants. On the other side of town, however, it is a different world entirely: Arabic-language signs, Lebanese coffee houses, and Yemeni mosques. Dearborn is as American a city as they come, but it is nevertheless different than most other American cities.

About forty thousand of Dearborn's one hundred thousand people are of Middle Eastern descent, and a great majority of them are Muslim. In Dearborn, it is as likely that you will see the minaret of a mosque as you will see a cross on a church. In fact, many fast-food restaurants serve burgers, sandwiches, and hot dogs made with halal meat. Dearborn has perhaps the largest concentration of Arabs in the world outside of the Middle East. Muslims of many different origins are also thriving in dozens of communities nationwide and in Canada.

The Islamic Center of America mosque, in Dearborn, Michigan, is pictured here on the evening of November 3, 2005, the night of *Eid ul-Fitr*.

From big cities like New York to smaller, less likely enclaves like Toledo, Ohio, Muslim Americans are thriving in the United States. By some estimates, their numbers, currently around six to seven million, are roughly the same as that of Jewish Americans. Muslims throughout America, whether recently arrived or sixth generation, are part of the rich mosaic of a nation built by immigrants. How they relate to this increasingly pluralistic society is a story that could be unfolding in a neighborhood near you.

Dearborn: A Center of Muslim Life

Many waves of immigration fed the ranks of Dearborn's Muslim community. Some arrived as early as the late nineteenth century, when Lebanese immigrants first started moving into the city. Many of these immigrants were Christian Arabs, followed later by their Muslim countrymen. Years later, more immigrants arrived: Palestinians, Iraqis, and more Lebanese, many escaping war or political troubles at home. Searching for work, immigrants from Yemen also arrived. Dearborn's Muslim population originates from many nations and worships in a variety of ways.

Started in the 1930s, the Yemeni Zaydi Dearborn Mosque was only the second mosque ever to be constructed in the United States. For non-Muslims, it perhaps most closely resembles what they imagine mosques are like in Arab Muslim nations like Yemen or Saudi Arabia. Services and the call to prayer are only in Arabic, and there are separate sections for men and women. In some local mosques, women pray behind the men or in separate rooms.

Many of the mosque's worshippers are local Yemenis, who tend to be more conservative than other Dearborn Muslims. It is rare to see Yemeni women out in public or in the neighborhood coffee houses where men gather. Many Yemenis avoid the more provocative aspects of American culture—violent and sexually explicit films, racy fashions, or leisure activities like going to bars and clubs.

In other parts of town, you see a different way of life. Mosques such as the Islamic Center of America, a Shia mosque that also welcomes Sunni Muslims as well as Muslims from all walks of life, have given women a larger say in the religious life of their community and have sought to connect with the society at-large through interfaith

The Perrysburg, Ohio–based Islamic Center of Greater Toledo is known for its open-door policy and good relations with its non-Muslim neighbors.

dialogue and civic involvement. This is a story unfolding in other parts of the United States, too.

Mosque on the Ohio Horizon

Drive on Interstate 75 through Ohio, and you will encounter an unusual sight outside of Toledo—the Islamic Center of Greater Toledo (located in Perrysburg, Ohio), a large, classical white mosque rising from the American heartland. Inside this impressive building, the attitude is more relaxed than in many mosques in the Middle East or in the insular Yemeni sections of Dearborn. Men and women pray in the same room, with only a small partition dividing them. It was also one of the first mosques to elect a woman as president.

A Progressive Tradition

The Islamic Center originally grew out of the local Syrian and Lebanese communities, which have roots going back more than seventy-five years. Sunnis and Shias representing twenty-three nationalities worship there. The Egyptian-born imam, Farooq Aboelzahab, told the *Christian Science*

Monitor that even he had to adjust to the mosque's very open atmosphere. "I had to learn from the last imam how to be more open-minded, more flexible, and to compromise on little things and focus on important issues," he said, adding, "We try to knock down this kind of division and teach mainstream Islam."

This has become harder lately, said S. Amjad Hussain, a university professor and center worshipper. "Whenever a community feels besieged they turn to religion," he told the *Christian Science Monitor*. "After 9/11 . . . American Muslims feel besieged and many become more orthodox and practicing . . . Some people in our center would like to reverse certain traditions, like that short partition between men and women."

The center has even become a tourist attraction, with visitors popping in when they see it from the highway. Most impressively, the local non-Muslim community has rallied around its Muslim neighbors during the war on terror. When nineteen Muslim hijackers killed thousands in terrorist attacks on September 11, 2001, Muslim Americans were as shocked as anyone else in America. Yet, prejudice against them and heightened security by police and other government officials increased greatly, including physical and verbal attacks by some Americans. When someone shot out a stained-glass window at Toledo's Islamic Center the night of September 11, local Christians decided to gather to pray for its protection. With three hundred expected to show, more than 1,500 sympathetic Christians linked hands to encircle the building that evening.

A Teaching Moment

Muslim Americans have taken the opportunity afforded by post-9/11 attention to educate non-Muslims about their religion and to remain steadfast in the face of these hardships. Many Muslims were inspired to learn more about their own religion and reach out to non-Muslims.

Imran Hafiz, a high school student in Phoenix, Arizona, told the *Christian Science Monitor* in January 2008, "I went to bed on September 10th an American, and on September 11th, I became a Muslim in people's minds." Some of his friends did not want him to play soccer with them anymore, calling him names like "Taliban," referring to the rulers of Afghanistan who had allied themselves with Osama bin Laden.

Rather than feeling down, Hafiz decided to educate others, while simultaneously helping Muslim teenagers to be proud of their religion, confront prejudice, and deal with their unique issues. With his mother, Dilara, and older sister, Yasmine, he spent nearly five years surveying Muslim teens. Eventually, they published *The American Muslim Teenager's Handbook*. Along with guides on how to pray and read the Qur'an, the book counsels teens on how to deal with issues like drinking, drugs, dating, and dancing. Educators—not just Muslims, but Jews, Christians, and others—are adding the book to school curricula. Dilara Hafiz said that when they contacted private Muslim schools in the United States, "The response we received expressed a desire for more guidance for teens from the mainstream, moderate viewpoint." Imran added, "It's been great—I've never felt so proud or open about my faith, and people are genuinely interested."

Back to Basics:
A New Muslim Identity

Many Muslims responded to the anger, fear, and distrust directed toward them after 9/11 by drawing closer together. An Iraqi-born mother who had long ago given up wearing a hijab was surprised to see her daughter start wearing one. Muslim student associations in high schools and colleges across North America became more popular.

In the post-9/11 climate, such actions were misinterpreted. Some Americans saw it as radical Islam growing, but the reality was more complicated—and more positive. A young Muslim woman in California, named Rehan, decided to adopt the hijab. "After I covered, I changed," she told the *Washington Post*. "I felt I wanted people to know how happy I am to be Muslim." Not everyone understood, however. A man in a supermarket told her that she would be more attractive without "that thing on your head. It's demeaning to women."

Muslims at Work

This return to religious practice can also seem like Muslims are separating themselves from the mainstream, while in many ways they are integrating. For example, many businesses are setting up spaces for prayer or becoming more flexible when it comes to granting days off for Islamic holidays. They recognize that they can attract young Muslim talent to work for them. For instance, Ford Motor

Fatima Kobeissi and Hyatt Bakri (*pictured left and right, respectively, wearing hijabs*) warm up before a Fordson High School basketball game in Dearborn, Michigan, on December 4, 2007.

Company, with its headquarters in Dearborn, has even hosted *iftar* dinners—the traditional breaking of the day-long fast during the thirty days of Ramadan—for the past seven years. Such actions reflect a general American trend toward providing reasonable religious accommodation to all employees as needed.

The Way Forward

Many non-Muslims are unfamiliar with the mainstream teachings of Islam, and many Muslims seek to integrate their religious life in contemporary societies, leading to mutual fear and animosity. But there are opportunities for education and acceptance starting to blossom everywhere. Rabbi Marc Schneier of New York, founder of the Foundation for Ethnic Understanding, organized a national summit that brought together Muslim Imams and Jewish rabbis early in 2007, a good sign that dialogue is possible.

In light of the sometimes-bitter contemporary divisions between Jews and Muslims, Schneier told the *Christian Science Monitor*, "The challenge is to try to strengthen Jewish-Muslim cooperation and have it serve as a paradigm for communities around the world." Ingrid Mattson, the first female president of the Islamic Society of North America, agreed, saying, "We need to get the truth about each other from one another."

It is an example that could well help Muslims and non-Muslims around the world, not just between Muslim communities and their neighbors in multicultural societies, but also between majority-Muslim nations and the West. There are many issues pertaining to Muslim countries that remain complex and controversial: the impact of the "War on Terror," the occupation of Iraq by the United States, the hostility between Israel and the Palestinians, and differing social and cultural norms. It is a big task for leaders, educators, activists, and normal citizens to help heal the wounds of prejudice and history. The work to be done is not only in some faraway place, but in a classroom near you or even right next door.

GLOSSARY

Alevis A minority branch of Shia Islam, mainly found in Turkey.

alms Anything donated to the poor or needy, such as food or money.

ayatollah Among Shias, the highest rank of scholars who have an extensive knowledge of Islamic law and who are major religious leaders in the community.

fundamentalist A term often used in the media to describe a person who adheres strictly to a given religion; many fundamentalists oppose secularism.

halal Describes meat that is slaughtered and prepared according to Islamic laws.

hijab A head scarf worn by Muslim women as a sign of piety and modesty.

imam A Muslim religious leader, including the leader or preacher of a mosque.

Moors A term used historically in Europe for the Muslims who ruled parts of North Africa, Spain, and Portugal during the Middle Ages.

mosque An Islamic house of worship.

mullah A title for a leader or teacher who is knowledgeable about Islam.

niqab A face veil worn by Muslim women.

Ottoman Turks The dynasty of Turks that ruled a Muslim empire that once extended from central Europe, through

Africa and the Middle East, from the fourteenth to the twentieth centuries.

sect A term for a sub-group of people with particular beliefs belonging to a religious tradition shared by other sub-groups.

secular A term referring to human activities or institutions that exclude religious motivations or influence.

Sharia A term signifying God's Law, which Muslim scholars throughout history have attempted to determine based on teachings in the Qur'an and the Sunnah of Muhammad.

Shia One of the two main branches of Islam; this branch does not accept the first three caliphs as the rightful heirs of Muhammad, and only considers Ali (the fourth caliph) and his descendants to be the true heirs.

Sunnah The life example of Muhammad, as reported in accounts (*hadith*) from many of his followers that were compiled after his death.

Sunni One of the two main branches of Islam, comprising the majority (roughly 85 percent) of all Muslims. Sunni Muslims accept the first four caliphs as the proper successors of the prophet Muhammad and have generally considered religious authority to be separate from the political authority of dynasties in history.

FOR MORE INFORMATION

American Muslim Alliance (AMA)
39675 Cedar Boulevard, Suite 220 E
Newark, CA 94560
(510) 252-9858
Web site: http://www.amaweb.org
The AMA seeks to gain a bigger political voice for U.S. Muslims.

Islamic Assembly of North America (IANA)
PMB #270
3588 Plymouth Road
Ann Arbor, MI 48105
Web site: http://www.iananet.org
This organization unifies many Muslim groups to promote cooperation, education, and activism within the North American Muslim community.

Islamic Institute of Toronto
1630 Neilson Road
Scarborough, ON M1X 1S3
Canada
(416) 335-9173
Web site: http://www.islam.ca
This nonprofit educational institute seeks to educate Muslim and non-Muslim Canadians about Islam.

Islamic Society of North America (ISNA)
P.O. Box 38
Plainfield, IN 46168
(317) 839-8157
Web site: http://www.isna.net
The ISNA seeks to educate North American Muslims and promote cooperation with other faiths and peoples.

Muslim American Society
P.O. Box 1896
Falls Church, VA 22041
(703) 998-6525
Web site: http://www.masnet.org
This nonprofit organization centers on charity and education.

Muslim Public Affairs Council (MPAC)
3010 Wilshire Boulevard, # 217
Los Angeles, CA 90010
(213) 383-3443; (213) 383-9674
Web site: http://www.mpac.org
MPAC works to help American Muslims with issues of civil rights, integration, and political representation.

Muslim Students Association National (MSAN) of the United States and Canada
P.O. Box 1096
Falls Church, VA 22041
(703) 820-7900
Web site: http://www.msanational.org

The MSAN promotes and helps link Muslim student associations on college and university campuses throughout North America.

National Iranian American Council (NIAC)
1411 K Street NW, Suite 600
Washington DC 20005
(202) 386-6325; (202) 386-6409
Web site: http://www.niacouncil.org
NIAC promotes the interests of Iranian Americans and helps them participate in civic and political life.

**The Prince Alwaleed Center for
Muslim-Christian Understanding**
Georgetown University
ICC 260
3700 O Street NW
Washington, DC 20057
(202) 687-8375
Web site: http://cmcu.georgetown.edu
This Georgetown University center of learning specializes in Muslim and Muslim-Christian issues and initiatives.

Web Sites
Due to the changing nature of Internet links, Rosen Publishing has developed an online list of Web sites related to the subject of this book. This site is updated regularly. Please use this link to access this list:

http://www.rosenlinks.com/ui/mawt

FOR FURTHER READING

Alkouatli, Claire. *Islam* (World Religions). New York, NY: Benchmark Books, 2006.

Barnes, Trevor. *Islam* (World Faiths). Boston, MA: Kingfisher Books, 2005.

Ganeri, Anita. *Muslim Festivals Throughout the Year* (A Year of Festivals Series). Mankato, MN: Smart Apple Media, 2003.

Hafiz, Dilara, Imran Hafiz, and Yasmine Hafiz. *The American Muslim Teenager's Handbook*. Phoenix, AZ: Acacia Publishing, 2007.

Hollihan-Elliot, Sheila. *Muslims in China* (The Growth and Influence of Islam in the Nations of Asia and Central Asia). Broomall, PA: Mason Crest Publishers, 2005.

Ibrahim, Muhammad, and Anita Ganeri. *Muslim Prayer and Worship*. North Mankato, MN: Sea to Sea Publications, 2008.

Moezzi, Melody. *War on Error: Real Stories of American Muslims*. Fayetteville, AK: University of Arkansas Press, 2007.

Patel, Mohammad. *Muslims in India* (The Growth and Influence of Islam in the Nations of Asia and Central Asia). Broomall, PA: Mason Crest Publishers, 2006.

Self, David. *Islam* (Religions of the World). Strongsville, OH: World Almanac Library, 2006.

BIBLIOGRAPHY

Abdo, Geneive. *Mecca and Main Street: Muslim Life in America After 9/11*. New York, NY: Oxford University Press, 2007.

America.gov. "Muslim Employees Find 'Welcome' Sign in U.S. Companies." October 25, 2007. Retrieved February 2008 (http://www.america.gov/st/ washfile-english/2007/October/20071025164409 xlrennef0.436413.html).

Anjani, Karima. "Farewell, Miss Indonesia: Plan to Outlaw the Miniskirt and the Bikini." *New York Sun*, May 10, 2006. Retrieved January 2008 (http://www.nysun.com/ article/32498).

Applebaum, Anne. "Multicultural Manners." Slate.com, October 24, 2006. Retrieved January 2008 (http://www. slate.com/id/2152031).

Arnove, Anthony. "Islam's Divided Crescent." *Nation*, July 8, 2002. Retrieved February 2008 (http://www.thenation. com/doc/20020708/arnove/2).

Azis, Dévina Fitriyanti. E-mail interview. February 27, 2008.

Bayoumi, Ayaa. "Religious Freedom: Muslims in Europe Face Widespread Abuse." *International Herald Tribune*, January 8, 2004. Retrieved February 2008 (http://www.iht.com/articles/2004/01/08/edbayoumi_ ed3_.php).

BBC News. "In Quotes: French Muslim Voices." November 11, 2005. Retrieved February 2008 (http://news.bbc.co.uk/2/hi/europe/4376500.stm).

BBC News. "Islam Tests Secular Istanbul." October 7, 2005. Retrieved January 2008 (http://news.bbc.co.uk/1/hi/world/europe/4312482.stm).

Beech, Hannah. "Why Indonesia Matters." *Time*, February 22, 2007. Retrieved February 2008 (http://www.time.com/time/magazine/article/0,9171,1592576,00.html).

Belton, Patrick. "In the Way of the Prophet: Ideologies and Institutions in Dearborn, Michigan, America's Muslim Capitol." AmericanCity.org, October 2003. Retrieved February 2008 (http://americancity.org/article.php?id_article=72).

Clausen, Lisa. "Meet the Neighbors." *Time*, September 7, 2004. Retrieved January 2008 (http://www.time.com/time/magazine/article/0,9171,693845,00.html).

Donovan, Jeffrey. "Turkey: A Divided Country Struggles for Identity." Radio Free Europe/Radio Liberty, May 3, 2007. Retrieved February 2008 (http://www.rferl.org/featuresarticle/2007/05/5EEE6EDF-7447-4D08-BF9F-68E2442F2F83.html).

Donovan, Jeffrey. "Turkey: Islam, Secularism Clash in Presidential Elections." Radio Free Europe/Radio Liberty, April 30, 2007. Retrieved February 2008 (http://www.rferl.org/featuresarticle/2007/04/ba34e394-713a-442e-b837d2e53b987728.html).

Elegant, Simon. "From Anger to Tolerance." *Time*, September 6, 2004. Retrieved January 2008 (http://www.time.com/time/magazine/article/0,9171, 692960,00.html).

Esposito, John L., and Dalia Mogahed. *Who Speaks for Islam?: What a Billion Muslims Really Think.* New York, NY: Gallup Press, 2008.

Glazov, Jaime. "Symposium: One Islam?" *FrontPage Magazine*, April 13, 2007. Retrieved February 2008 (http://www.frontpagemag.com/Articles/ReadArticle. asp?ID=27847).

Grieshaber, Kirsten. "Tempers Flare in German Mosque Dispute." Associated Press, July 4, 2007. Retrieved January 2008 (http://www.washingtonpost.com/ wp-dyn/content/article/2007/07/04/ AR2007070400814.html).

Haddad, Yvonne Yazbeck, ed. *Muslims in the West: From Sojourners to Citizens.* New York, NY: Oxford University Press, 2002.

Haddad, Yvonne Yazbeck, Jane I. Smith, and Kathleen M. Moore. *Muslim Women in America: The Challenge of Islamic Identity Today.* New York, NY: Oxford University Press, 2006.

Kepel, Gilles. *The War for Muslim Minds: Islam and the West.* Translated by Pascale Ghazaleh. Cambridge, MA: Belknap Press, 2006.

Markey, Sean. "Middle East Expert Discusses Islamic Extremism." *National Geographic News*, December 11, 2002. Retrieved January 2008 (http://news. nationalgeographic.com/news/2002/12/1211_ 021211_mideast.html).

McAllister, J. F. O. "Hate Around the Corner." *Time*, July 17, 2005. Retrieved January 2008 (http://www.time.com/time/magazine/article/0,9171,1083866,00.html).

McAllister, J. F. O. "The Terrorists Next Door." *Time*, August 1, 2005. Retrieved January 2008 (http://www.time.com/time/magazine/article/0,9171,1088721,00.html).

Nonneman, Gerd, et al., eds. *Muslim Communities in the New Europe*. Ithaca, NY: Ithaca Press, 1998.

Powell, Bill. "Struggle for the Soul of Islam." *Time*, September 13, 2004. Retrieved January 2008 (http://www.time.com/time/magazine/article/0,9171,995071,00.html).

Power, Carla. "Baring Our Selves." *Time*, October 4, 2007. Retrieved January 2008 (http://www.time.com/time/magazine/article/0,9171,1668236,00.html).

Purvis, Andrew. "Divided They Stand." *Time*, May 3, 2007. Retrieved January 2008 (http://www.time.com/time/magazine/article/0,9171,1617173,00.html).

Sanders, Bi. "Interpreting Veils: Meanings Have Changed with Politics, History." *Seattle Weekly*, May 27, 2003. Retrieved January 2008 (http://seattletimes.nwsource.com/news/nation-world/infocus/mideast/islam/interpreting_veils.html).

Sardar, Ziauddin. *What Do Muslims Believe?: The Roots and Realities of Modern Islam*. New York, NY: Walker & Co., 2007.

INDEX

About the Author

Philip Wolny is a writer and editor currently finishing an M.A. in European studies at Jagiellonian University in Krakow, Poland. He has long been fascinated by the Muslim world and has done extensive research on it for his masters thesis, which focuses on the political and cultural assimilation of citizens of Muslim descent in France.

About the Consultant

Munir Shaikh oversees research and consulting activities at the Institute on Religion and Civic Values (IRCV), a non-advocacy organization with expertise in world religions, world history, civil society, pluralism, and related subjects. Munir has a Master's degree in Islamic Studies from the University of California, Los Angeles, and has over fifteen years of experience in writing and editing texts pertaining to Islamic history and culture.

Photo Credits

Cover (bottom left) Bay Ismoyo/AFP/Getty Images; cover (bottom right) Melanie Stetson Freeman/*The Christian Science Monitor*/Getty Images, pp. 4–5 Richard Ross/The Image Bank/Getty Images; p. 9 Jewel Samad/AFP/Getty Images; p. 11 Dewira/AFP/Getty Images; p. 13 Robert F. Sisson/*National Geographic*/Getty Images; p. 15 Bay Ismoyo/AFP/Getty Images; p. 18 Mohammed Abed/AFP/Getty Images; p. 21 Gabriel Duval/AFP/Getty Images; pp. 23, 39, 42, 50 © AP Images; p. 26 Simon Roberts/Reportage/Getty Images; p. 30 Christopher Furlong/Getty Images; p. 33 Bruno Vincent/Getty Images; p. 35 Henning Kaiser/AFP/Getty Images; p. 41 Herman Agopian/Taxi/Getty Images; p. 44 Bill Pugliano/Getty Images; p. 46 Melanie Stetson Freeman/*The Christian Science Monitor*/Getty Images.

Designer: Les Kanturek; Photo Researcher: Amy Feinberg